THIS JOURNAL BELONGS TO

....

WEEK 1

Space For My Thoughts

Happiness never decreases
by being shared

— Gautama Buddha

I Am Grateful For...

MONDAY

....
....
....
....

TUESDAY

....
....
....
....

WEDNESDAY

....
....
....
....

THURSDAY

....
....
....
....

FRIDAY

....
....
....
....

SATURDAY

....
....
....
....

SUNDAY

....
....
....
....

◇—— REFLECTION SECTION ——◇

This week I mostly felt...

UNHAPPY   HAPPY :D

1   2   3   4   5 | 6   7   8   9   10

Highlight of my week

....
....
....
....
....

Person of the week

....
....

WEEK 2

Space For My Thoughts

I Am Grateful For...

MONDAY

....
....
....
....

TUESDAY

....
....
....
....

WEDNESDAY

....
....
....
....

THURSDAY

....
....
....
....

FRIDAY

....
....
....

SATURDAY

....
....
....
....

SUNDAY

....
....
....
....

❖ —— REFLECTION SECTION —— ❖

This week I mostly felt...

UNHAPPY   HAPPY :D

1   2   3   4   5 | 6   7   8   9   10

Highlight of my week

....
....
....
....
....
....
....

Person of the week

....
....

WEEK 3

Space For My Thoughts

I Am Grateful For...

MONDAY

....
....
....
....

TUESDAY

....
....
....
....

WEDNESDAY

....
....
....
....

THURSDAY

....
....
....
....

FRIDAY

....
....

SATURDAY

....
....
....
....

SUNDAY

....
....
....
....

REFLECTION SECTION

This week I mostly felt...

UNHAPPY | HAPPY :D

1 2 3 4 5 | 6 7 8 9 10

Highlight of my week

....
....
....
....
....

Person of the week

....

WEEK 4

Space For My Thoughts

I Am Grateful For...

Monday

....
....
....
....

Tuesday

....
....
....
....

Wednesday

....
....
....
....

Thursday

....
....
....
....

Friday

....
....
....

Saturday

....
....
....
....

Sunday

....
....
....
....

❖ —— Reflection Section —— ❖

This week I mostly felt...

UNHAPPY | HAPPY :D

1   2   3   4   5 | 6   7   8   9   10

Highlight of my week

....
....
....
....
....
....

Person of the week

....

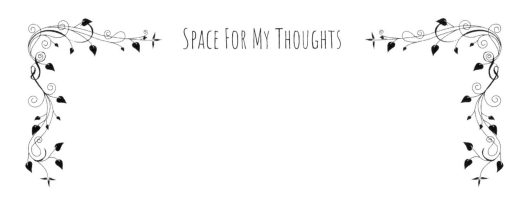

SPACE FOR MY THOUGHTS

> Happiness is where we find it, but rarely where we seek it

— Jean Antoine Petit-Senn

I Am Grateful For...

MONDAY

....

....

....

....

TUESDAY

....

....

....

....

WEDNESDAY

....

....

....

....

THURSDAY

....

....

....

....

FRIDAY

....

....

....

....

SATURDAY

....

....

....

....

SUNDAY

....

....

....

....

⟶ REFLECTION SECTION ⟵

This week I mostly felt...

UNHAPPY   HAPPY :D

1   2   3   4   5 | 6   7   8   9   10

Highlight of my week

....

....

....

....

....

Person of the week

....

WEEK 6

Space For My Thoughts

I Am Grateful For...

Monday
....
....
....
....

Tuesday
....
....
....
....

Wednesday
....
....
....
....

Thursday
....
....
....
....

Friday
....
....
....
....

Saturday
....
....
....
....

Sunday
....
....
....
....

⬥ Reflection Section ⬥

This week I mostly felt...

UNHAPPY   HAPPY :D

1   2   3   4   5 | 6   7   8   9   10

Highlight of my week
....
....
....
....
....

Person of the week
....

WEEK 7

Space For My Thoughts

I Am Grateful For...

MONDAY

....

....

....

....

TUESDAY

....

....

....

....

WEDNESDAY

....

....

....

....

THURSDAY

....

....

....

....

FRIDAY

....

....

....

SATURDAY

....

....

....

....

SUNDAY

....

....

....

....

REFLECTION SECTION

This week I mostly felt...

UNHAPPY						HAPPY :D			
1	2	3	4	5	6	7	8	9	10

Highlight of my week

....

....

....

....

....

....

Person of the week

....

WEEK 8

SPACE FOR MY THOUGHTS

I Am Grateful For...

MONDAY

....
....
....
....

TUESDAY

....
....
....
....

WEDNESDAY

....
....
....
....

THURSDAY

....
....
....
....

FRIDAY

....
....
....
....

SATURDAY

....
....
....
....

SUNDAY

....
....
....
....

◇— REFLECTION SECTION —◇

This week I mostly felt...

UNHAPPY   HAPPY :D

1   2   3   4   5 | 6   7   8   9   10

Highlight of my week

....
....
....
....
....

Person of the week

....

Space For My Thoughts

"

I am a slow walker, but I never walk back

— Abraham Lincoln

I Am Grateful For...

Monday

....
....
....
....

Tuesday

....
....
....
....

Wednesday

....
....
....
....

Thursday

....
....
....
....

Friday

....
....
....
....

Saturday

....
....
....
....

Sunday

....
....
....
....

⬦— Reflection Section —⬦

This week I mostly felt...

UNHAPPY | HAPPY :D

1 2 3 4 5 | 6 7 8 9 10

Highlight of my week

....
....
....
....
....
....

Person of the week

WEEK 10

Space For My Thoughts

I Am Grateful For...

Monday

....
....
....
....

Tuesday

....
....
....
....

Wednesday

....
....
....
....

Thursday

....
....
....
....

Friday

....
....

Saturday

....
....
....
....

Sunday

....
....
....
....

Reflection Section

This week I mostly felt...

UNHAPPY   HAPPY :D

1   2   3   4   5 | 6   7   8   9   10

Highlight of my week

....
....
....
....
....

Person of the week

....
....

WEEK 11

Space For My Thoughts

I Am Grateful For...

Monday

....
....
....
....

Tuesday

....
....
....
....

Wednesday

....
....
....
....

Thursday

....
....
....
....

Friday

....
....
....

Saturday

....
....
....
....

Sunday

....
....
....
....

Reflection Section

This week I mostly felt...

UNHAPPY   HAPPY :D

1   2   3   4   5 | 6   7   8   9   10

Highlight of my week

....
....
....
....
....

Person of the week

....

WEEK 12

SPACE FOR MY THOUGHTS

I Am Grateful For...

MONDAY

....
....
....
....

TUESDAY

....
....
....
....

WEDNESDAY

....
....
....
....

THURSDAY

....
....
....
....

FRIDAY

....
....
....
....

SATURDAY

....
....
....
....

SUNDAY

....
....
....
....

◆— REFLECTION SECTION —◆

This week I mostly felt...

UNHAPPY   HAPPY :D

1   2   3   4   5 | 6   7   8   9   10

Highlight of my week

....
....
....
....
....

Person of the week

....

Space For My Thoughts

Persistent people begin their success
where others end in failure

— Edward Eggleston

I Am Grateful For...

MONDAY

....

....

....

....

TUESDAY

....

....

....

....

WEDNESDAY

....

....

....

....

THURSDAY

....

....

....

....

FRIDAY

....

....

....

SATURDAY

....

....

....

....

SUNDAY

....

....

....

....

REFLECTION SECTION

This week I mostly felt...

UNHAPPY   HAPPY :D

1   2   3   4   5 | 6   7   8   9   10

Highlight of my week

....

....

....

....

....

....

Person of the week

WEEK 14

SPACE FOR MY THOUGHTS

I Am Grateful For...

Monday

....
....
....
....

Tuesday

....
....
....

Wednesday

....
....
....
....

Thursday

....
....
....

Friday

....
....
....

Saturday

....
....
....
....

Sunday

....
....
....

⟶ — Reflection Section — ⟵

This week I mostly felt...

UNHAPPY   HAPPY :D

1   2   3   4   5 | 6   7   8   9   10

Highlight of my week

....
....
....
....
....

Person of the week

....

WEEK 15

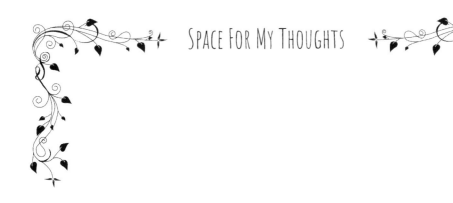

SPACE FOR MY THOUGHTS

I Am Grateful For...

Monday

....
....
....
....

Tuesday

....
....
....
....

Wednesday

....
....
....
....

Thursday

....
....
....

Friday

....
....
....

Saturday

....
....
....
....

Sunday

....
....
....
....

Reflection Section

This week I mostly felt...

UNHAPPY   HAPPY :D

1   2   3   4   5 | 6   7   8   9   10

Highlight of my week

....
....
....
....
....

Person of the week

WEEK 16

Space For My Thoughts

I Am Grateful For...

MONDAY

....

....

....

....

TUESDAY

....

....

....

....

WEDNESDAY

....

....

....

....

THURSDAY

....

....

....

....

FRIDAY

....

....

....

SATURDAY

....

....

....

....

SUNDAY

....

....

....

....

REFLECTION SECTION

This week I mostly felt...

UNHAPPY   HAPPY :D

1   2   3   4   5 | 6   7   8   9   10

Highlight of my week

....

....

....

....

....

Person of the week

....

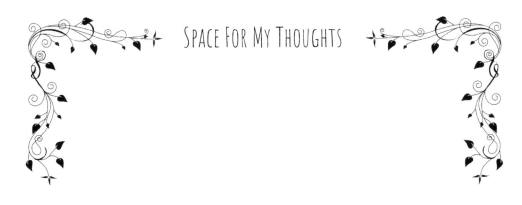

SPACE FOR MY THOUGHTS

"

Happiness is as a butterfly which, when pursued, is always beyond our grasp, but which if you will sit down quietly, may alight upon you

— Nathaniel Hawthorne

I Am Grateful For...

Monday

....
....
....
....

Tuesday

....
....
....
....

Wednesday

....
....
....
....

Thursday

....
....
....
....

Friday

....
....
....

Saturday

....
....
....
....

Sunday

....
....
....
....

Reflection Section

This week I mostly felt...

UNHAPPY | HAPPY :D

1   2   3   4   5 | 6   7   8   9   10

Highlight of my week

....
....
....
....
....
....

Person of the week

....

WEEK 18

Space For My Thoughts

I Am Grateful For...

Monday

....
....
....
....

Tuesday

....
....
....
....

Wednesday

....
....
....
....

Thursday

....
....
....
....

Friday

....
....
....
....

Saturday

....
....
....
....

Sunday

....
....
....
....

Reflection Section

This week I mostly felt...

UNHAPPY   HAPPY :D

1   2   3   4   5 | 6   7   8   9   10

Highlight of my week

....
....
....
....
....

Person of the week

....
....

WEEK 19

SPACE FOR MY THOUGHTS

I Am Grateful For...

Monday

....

....

....

....

Tuesday

....

....

....

....

Wednesday

....

....

....

....

Thursday

....

....

....

....

Friday

....

....

....

Saturday

....

....

....

....

Sunday

....

....

....

....

❖—— Reflection Section ——❖

This week I mostly felt...

UNHAPPY   HAPPY :D

1   2   3   4   5 | 6   7   8   9   10

Highlight of my week

....

....

....

....

....

Person of the week

....

WEEK 20

Space For My Thoughts

I Am Grateful For...

MONDAY

....

....

....

....

TUESDAY

....

....

....

....

WEDNESDAY

....

....

....

....

THURSDAY

....

....

....

....

FRIDAY

....

....

....

SATURDAY

....

....

....

....

SUNDAY

....

....

....

....

REFLECTION SECTION

This week I mostly felt...

UNHAPPY   HAPPY :D

1   2   3   4   5 | 6   7   8   9   10

Highlight of my week

....

....

....

....

....

....

Person of the week

....

WEEK 21

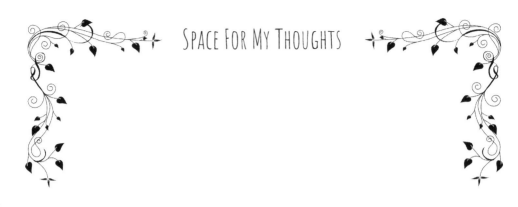

Space For My Thoughts

Happiness depends more on the inward
disposition of mind than on outward
circumstances

— Benjamin Franklin

I Am Grateful For...

MONDAY

....

....

....

....

TUESDAY

....

....

....

....

WEDNESDAY

....

....

....

....

THURSDAY

....

....

....

....

FRIDAY

....

....

....

SATURDAY

....

....

....

....

SUNDAY

....

....

....

....

REFLECTION SECTION

This week I mostly felt...

UNHAPPY   HAPPY :D

1   2   3   4   5 | 6   7   8   9   10

Highlight of my week

....

....

....

....

....

Person of the week

....

WEEK 22

Space For My Thoughts

I Am Grateful For...

Monday

....
....
....
....

Tuesday

....
....
....
....

Wednesday

....
....
....
....

Thursday

....
....
....
....

Friday

....
....

Saturday

....
....
....
....

Sunday

....
....
....
....

Reflection Section

This week I mostly felt...

UNHAPPY   HAPPY :D

1   2   3   4   5 | 6   7   8   9   10

Highlight of my week

....
....
....
....
....

Person of the week

....

WEEK 23

SPACE FOR MY THOUGHTS

I Am Grateful For...

Monday

....
....
....
....

Tuesday

....
....
....
....

Wednesday

....
....
....
....

Thursday

....
....
....
....

Friday

....
....
....
....

Saturday

....
....
....
....

Sunday

....
....
....
....

Reflection Section

This week I mostly felt...

UNHAPPY   HAPPY :D

1   2   3   4   5 | 6   7   8   9   10

Highlight of my week

....
....
....
....
....
....

Person of the week

....
....

WEEK 24

Space For My Thoughts

I Am Grateful For...

Monday

....
....
....
....

Tuesday

....
....
....
....

Wednesday

....
....
....
....

Thursday

....
....
....
....

Friday

....
....
....

Saturday

....
....
....
....

Sunday

....
....
....
....

Reflection Section

This week I mostly felt...

UNHAPPY   HAPPY :D

1   2   3   4   5 | 6   7   8   9   10

Highlight of my week

....
....
....
....
....
....
....

Person of the week

....

WEEK 25

SPACE FOR MY THOUGHTS

"

Have patience with all things, But, first of all with yourself

— Saint Francis De Sales

I Am Grateful For...

Monday

....
....
....
....

Tuesday

....
....
....
....

Wednesday

....
....
....
....

Thursday

....
....
....
....

Friday

....
....

Saturday

....
....
....
....

Sunday

....
....
....
....

Reflection Section

This week I mostly felt...

UNHAPPY   HAPPY :D

1   2   3   4   5 | 6   7   8   9   10

Highlight of my week

....
....
....
....
....

Person of the week

....

WEEK 26

SPACE FOR MY THOUGHTS

I Am Grateful For...

Monday

....
....
....
....

Tuesday

....
....
....
....

Wednesday

....
....
....
....

Thursday

....
....
....
....

Friday

....
....
....

Saturday

....
....
....
....

Sunday

....
....
....
....

Reflection Section

This week I mostly felt...

UNHAPPY | HAPPY :D

1   2   3   4   5   6   7   8   9   10

Highlight of my week

....
....
....
....
....
....

Person of the week

WEEK 27

SPACE FOR MY THOUGHTS

I Am Grateful For...

Monday

....
....
....
....

Tuesday

....
....
....
....

Wednesday

....
....
....
....

Thursday

....
....
....
....

Friday

....
....
....
....

Saturday

....
....
....
....

Sunday

....
....
....
....

Reflection Section

This week I mostly felt...

UNHAPPY | HAPPY :D

1 2 3 4 5 | 6 7 8 9 10

Highlight of my week

....
....
....
....
....
....
....

Person of the week

....

WEEK 28

Space For My Thoughts

I Am Grateful For...

Monday

....
....
....
....

Tuesday

....
....
....
....

Wednesday

....
....
....
....

Thursday

....
....
....
....

Friday

....
....
....

Saturday

....
....
....
....

Sunday

....
....
....
....

Reflection Section

This week I mostly felt...

UNHAPPY   HAPPY :D

1   2   3   4   5 | 6   7   8   9   10

Highlight of my week

....
....
....
....
....
....

Person of the week

....

WEEK 29

Space For My Thoughts

"

I am not discouraged, because every
wrong attempt discarded is another
step forward

— Thomas A. Edison

I Am Grateful For...

MONDAY

....
....
....
....

TUESDAY

....
....
....
....

WEDNESDAY

....
....
....
....

THURSDAY

....
....
....
....

FRIDAY

....
....
....

SATURDAY

....
....
....
....

SUNDAY

....
....
....
....

REFLECTION SECTION

This week I mostly felt...

UNHAPPY   HAPPY :D

1   2   3   4   5 | 6   7   8   9   10

Highlight of my week

....
....
....
....
....
....

Person of the week

WEEK 30

Space For My Thoughts

I Am Grateful For...

MONDAY

....

....

....

....

TUESDAY

....

....

....

....

WEDNESDAY

....

....

....

....

THURSDAY

....

....

....

....

FRIDAY

....

....

....

....

SATURDAY

....

....

....

....

SUNDAY

....

....

....

....

REFLECTION SECTION

This week I mostly felt...

UNHAPPY   HAPPY :D

1   2   3   4   5 | 6   7   8   9   10

Highlight of my week

....

....

....

....

....

....

Person of the week

....

WEEK 31

Space For My Thoughts

I Am Grateful For...

MONDAY

....

....

....

....

TUESDAY

....

....

....

....

WEDNESDAY

....

....

....

....

THURSDAY

....

....

....

....

FRIDAY

....

....

....

....

SATURDAY

....

....

....

....

SUNDAY

....

....

....

....

REFLECTION SECTION

This week I mostly felt...

UNHAPPY   HAPPY :D

1   2   3   4   5 | 6   7   8   9   10

Highlight of my week

....

....

....

....

....

....

Person of the week

....

....

WEEK 32

SPACE FOR MY THOUGHTS

I Am Grateful For...

MONDAY

....
....
....
....

TUESDAY

....
....
....
....

WEDNESDAY

....
....
....
....

THURSDAY

....
....
....

FRIDAY

....
....
....

SATURDAY

....
....
....
....

SUNDAY

....
....
....
....

REFLECTION SECTION

This week I mostly felt...

UNHAPPY | HAPPY :D

1 2 3 4 5 | 6 7 8 9 10

Highlight of my week

....
....
....
....
....
....

Person of the week

....

WEEK 33

SPACE FOR MY THOUGHTS

"

Use what talents you possess; the
woods would be very silent if no birds
sang there except those that sang best

— Henry Van Dyke

I Am Grateful For...

MONDAY

....
....
....
....

TUESDAY

....
....
....
....

WEDNESDAY

....
....
....
....

THURSDAY

....
....
....
....

FRIDAY

....
....
....

SATURDAY

....
....
....
....

SUNDAY

....
....
....
....

Reflection Section

This week I mostly felt...

UNHAPPY   HAPPY :D

1   2   3   4   5 | 6   7   8   9   10

Highlight of my week

....
....
....
....
....
....

Person of the week

....

WEEK 34

Space For My Thoughts

I Am Grateful For...

Monday

....
....
....
....

Tuesday

....
....
....
....

Wednesday

....
....
....
....

Thursday

....
....
....
....

Friday

....
....
....

Saturday

....
....
....
....

Sunday

....
....
....

⟨— REFLECTION SECTION —⟩

This week I mostly felt...

UNHAPPY   HAPPY :D

1   2   3   4   5 | 6   7   8   9   10

Highlight of my week

....
....
....
....
....

Person of the week

....

WEEK 35

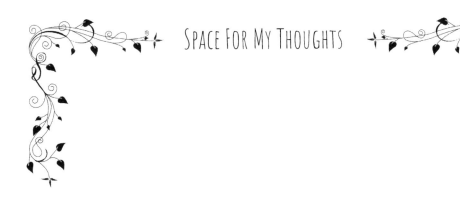

SPACE FOR MY THOUGHTS

I Am Grateful For...

Monday

....
....
....
....

Tuesday

....
....
....
....

Wednesday

....
....
....
....

Thursday

....
....
....
....

Friday

....
....
....

Saturday

....
....
....
....

Sunday

....
....
....

Reflection Section

This week I mostly felt...

UNHAPPY   HAPPY :D

1   2   3   4   5   6   7   8   9   10

Highlight of my week

....
....
....
....
....

Person of the week

....

WEEK 36

Space For My Thoughts

I Am Grateful For...

MONDAY

....
....
....
....

TUESDAY

....
....
....
....

WEDNESDAY

....
....
....
....

THURSDAY

....
....
....
....

FRIDAY

....
....
....
....

SATURDAY

....
....
....
....

SUNDAY

....
....
....
....

REFLECTION SECTION

This week I mostly felt...

UNHAPPY   HAPPY :D

1   2   3   4   5 | 6   7   8   9   10

Highlight of my week

....
....
....
....
....
....

Person of the week

....
....

SPACE FOR MY THOUGHTS

"

It is not how much we have, but how
much we enjoy, that makes happiness

— Charles Spurgeon

I Am Grateful For...

MONDAY

....
....
....
....

TUESDAY

....
....
....
....

WEDNESDAY

....
....
....
....

THURSDAY

....
....
....
....

FRIDAY

....
....
....
....

SATURDAY

....
....
....
....

SUNDAY

....
....
....
....

⟋ —— REFLECTION SECTION —— ⟍

This week I mostly felt...

UNHAPPY   HAPPY :D

1   2   3   4   5 | 6   7   8   9   10

Highlight of my week

....
....
....
....
....
....

Person of the week

....

WEEK 38

SPACE FOR MY THOUGHTS

I Am Grateful For...

Monday

....
....
....
....

Tuesday

....
....
....
....

Wednesday

....
....
....
....

Thursday

....
....
....
....

Friday

....
....
....

Saturday

....
....
....
....

Sunday

....
....
....

❖ Reflection Section ❖

This week I mostly felt...

UNHAPPY | HAPPY :D

1 2 3 4 5 | 6 7 8 9 10

Highlight of my week

....
....
....
....
....
....

Person of the week

....
....

WEEK 39

SPACE FOR MY THOUGHTS

I Am Grateful For...

MONDAY

....

....

....

....

TUESDAY

....

....

....

....

WEDNESDAY

....

....

....

....

THURSDAY

....

....

....

....

FRIDAY

....

....

....

....

SATURDAY

....

....

....

....

SUNDAY

....

....

....

....

◦—◦ REFLECTION SECTION ◦—◦

This week I mostly felt...

UNHAPPY   HAPPY :D

1   2   3   4   5 | 6   7   8   9   10

Highlight of my week

....

....

....

....

....

....

Person of the week

....

....

WEEK 40

SPACE FOR MY THOUGHTS

I Am Grateful For...

MONDAY

....
....
....
....

TUESDAY

....
....
....
....

WEDNESDAY

....
....
....
....

THURSDAY

....
....
....

FRIDAY

....
....
....

SATURDAY

....
....
....
....

SUNDAY

....
....
....
....

REFLECTION SECTION

This week I mostly felt...

UNHAPPY   HAPPY :D

1   2   3   4   5 | 6   7   8   9   10

Highlight of my week

....
....
....
....
....

Person of the week

....

SPACE FOR MY THOUGHTS

"

Let no feeling of discouragement prey upon you, and in the end you are sure to succeed

— Abraham Lincoln

I Am Grateful For...

MONDAY

....
....
....
....

TUESDAY

....
....
....
....

WEDNESDAY

....
....
....
....

THURSDAY

....
....
....
....

FRIDAY

....
....
....

SATURDAY

....
....
....
....

SUNDAY

....
....
....
....

⬥ Reflection Section ⬥

This week I mostly felt...

UNHAPPY   HAPPY :D

1   2   3   4   5 | 6   7   8   9   10

Highlight of my week

....
....
....
....

Person of the week

....

WEEK 42

Space For My Thoughts

I Am Grateful For...

MONDAY

....

....

....

....

TUESDAY

....

....

....

....

WEDNESDAY

....

....

....

....

THURSDAY

....

....

....

....

FRIDAY

....

....

SATURDAY

....

....

....

....

SUNDAY

....

....

....

....

REFLECTION SECTION

This week I mostly felt...

UNHAPPY   HAPPY :D

1   2   3   4   5 | 6   7   8   9   10

Highlight of my week

....

....

....

....

....

Person of the week

....

WEEK 43

Space For My Thoughts

I Am Grateful For...

Monday

....
....
....
....

Tuesday

....
....
....
....

Wednesday

....
....
....
....

Thursday

....
....
....
....

Friday

....
....
....

Saturday

....
....
....
....

Sunday

....
....
....
....

Reflection Section

This week I mostly felt...

UNHAPPY   HAPPY :D

1   2   3   4   5 | 6   7   8   9   10

Highlight of my week

....
....
....
....
....
....

Person of the week

....
....

WEEK 43

Space For My Thoughts

I Am Grateful For...

Monday

....

....

....

....

Tuesday

....

....

....

....

Wednesday

....

....

....

....

Thursday

....

....

....

....

Friday

....

....

....

Saturday

....

....

....

....

Sunday

....

....

....

....

Reflection Section

This week I mostly felt...

UNHAPPY   HAPPY :D

1   2   3   4   5 | 6   7   8   9   10

Highlight of my week

....

....

....

....

....

....

Person of the week

....

Space For My Thoughts

"

The drops of rain make a hole in the
stone, not by violence, but by oft falling

— Lucretius

I Am Grateful For...

Monday

....
....
....
....

Tuesday

....
....
....
....

Wednesday

....
....
....
....

Thursday

....
....
....
....

Friday

....
....
....
....

Saturday

....
....
....
....

Sunday

....
....
....
....

Reflection Section

This week I mostly felt...

UNHAPPY   HAPPY :D

1   2   3   4   5 | 6   7   8   9   10

Highlight of my week

....
....
....
....
....

Person of the week

....
....

WEEK 45

SPACE FOR MY THOUGHTS

I Am Grateful For...

Monday

....
....
....
....

Tuesday

....
....
....
....

Wednesday

....
....
....
....

Thursday

....
....
....
....

Friday

....
....
....
....

Saturday

....
....
....
....

Sunday

....
....
....
....

Reflection Section

This week I mostly felt...

UNHAPPY   HAPPY :D

1   2   3   4   5 | 6   7   8   9   10

Highlight of my week

....
....
....
....
....
....

Person of the week

....
....

WEEK 46

SPACE FOR MY THOUGHTS

I Am Grateful For...

Monday

....

....

....

....

Tuesday

....

....

....

....

Wednesday

....

....

....

....

Thursday

....

....

....

....

Friday

....

....

Saturday

....

....

....

....

Sunday

....

....

....

....

```
◇—— REFLECTION SECTION ——◇

This week I mostly felt...

UNHAPPY                    HAPPY :D

1   2   3   4   5 | 6   7   8   9   10

Highlight of my week

........................................................

........................................................

........................................................

........................................................

........................................................

........................................................

Person of the week

........................................................
```

WEEK 47

Space For My Thoughts

I Am Grateful For...

MONDAY

....

....

....

....

TUESDAY

....

....

....

....

WEDNESDAY

....

....

....

....

THURSDAY

....

....

....

....

FRIDAY

....

....

....

SATURDAY

....

....

....

....

SUNDAY

....

....

....

....

REFLECTION SECTION

This week I mostly felt...

UNHAPPY | HAPPY :D

1   2   3   4   5 | 6   7   8   9   10

Highlight of my week

....

....

....

....

....

....

....

Person of the week

....

Space For My Thoughts

"

For every minute you are angry you lose sixty seconds of happiness

— Ralph Waldo Emerson

I Am Grateful For...

Monday

....
....
....
....

Tuesday

....
....
....
....

Wednesday

....
....
....
....

Thursday

....
....
....
....

Friday

....
....

Saturday

....
....
....
....

Sunday

....
....
....
....

◇—— **Reflection Section** ——◇

This week I mostly felt...

UNHAPPY   HAPPY :D

1   2   3   4   5 | 6   7   8   9   10

Highlight of my week

....
....
....
....
....

Person of the week

....

WEEK 49

SPACE FOR MY THOUGHTS

I Am Grateful For...

Monday

....
....
....
....

Tuesday

....
....
....
....

Wednesday

....
....
....
....

Thursday

....
....
....
....

Friday

....
....
....

Saturday

....
....
....
....

Sunday

....
....
....
....

Reflection Section

This week I mostly felt...

UNHAPPY   HAPPY :D

1   2   3   4   5 | 6   7   8   9   10

Highlight of my week

....
....
....
....
....

Person of the week

....

WEEK 50

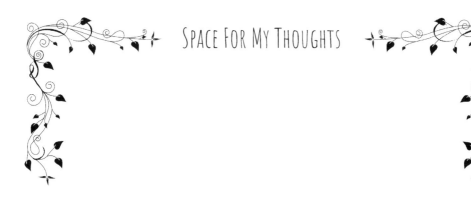

Space For My Thoughts

I Am Grateful For...

Monday

....

....

....

....

Tuesday

....

....

....

....

Wednesday

....

....

....

....

Thursday

....

....

....

....

Friday

....

....

....

....

Saturday

....

....

....

....

Sunday

....

....

....

....

Reflection Section

This week I mostly felt...

UNHAPPY   HAPPY :D

1   2   3   4   5 | 6   7   8   9   10

Highlight of my week

....

....

....

....

....

Person of the week

....

WEEK 51

Space For My Thoughts

I Am Grateful For...

Monday
....
....
....
....

Tuesday
....
....
....
....

Wednesday
....
....
....
....

Thursday
....
....
....
....

Friday
....
....
....

Saturday
....
....
....
....

Sunday
....
....
....
....

Reflection Section

This week I mostly felt...

UNHAPPY   HAPPY :D

1   2   3   4   5 | 6   7   8   9   10

Highlight of my week
....
....
....
....
....
....

Person of the week
....

SPACE FOR MY THOUGHTS

"

The drops of rain make a hole in the stone, not by violence, but by oft falling

— Lucretius

I Am Grateful For...

Monday
....
....
....
....

Tuesday
....
....
....
....

Wednesday
....
....
....
....

Thursday
....
....
....
....

Friday
....
....
....

Saturday
....
....
....
....

Sunday
....
....
....
....

✦ Reflection Section ✦

This week I mostly felt...

UNHAPPY   HAPPY :D

1   2   3   4   5 | 6   7   8   9   10

Highlight of my week
....
....
....
....
....
....

Person of the week
....
....